The Technology o

The Technology of Doing Creating & Being

by Monika K. Moss-Gransberry

Keys for Life Publishing
Cleveland Ohio
2017

The Technology of Doing Creating and Being

Published by Rolands Press and Keys For Life Publishing, Cleveland, Ohio

Edited by May K. Haugstad
Cover Art by Walter Allen Rogers Jr.
Graphic Designer Georgio Sabino III

Library of Congress Cataloging-in-publication Data

Moss-Gransberry, Monika, K. The Technology of Doing, Creating, and Being by Monika K. Moss-Gransberry
Includes index. ISBN- 978-0-9849520-1-4
1. Self-Help Book
--- ----- ----- ------- - -

Table of Contents

Monika Moss-Gransberry

Acknowledgements

I cannot thank everyone whose support has gotten me to this moment in my life... Especially my parents; my mom and editor, May, and my husband, Everett. My good friend, Connie Atkins for her proofreading skills and her wise counsel over the years. I thank my children, Kenny and Roland who taught me so much and pushed me to be my best self. My long time mentor and teacher, John Carter, and spiritual teacher, John Harris; thank you for your patience and love. Thanks to my friends and supporters whose hands and action made this book possible. I am so full of gratitude for all the spiritual guidance I received that gave me the understanding and the words used in this book. And I thank God for everything.

I used to cry out of longing for love, for happiness, for right relationships, for peace. Now I cry because I am eternally grateful for the learning and practice of these technologies as I have received them from spirit through my teachers and mentors. Now I cry because my every need is met and because of the intense joy that grows in me as all my prayers are being answered. I cry because that is an overwhelming experience. I cry because I see the light at the end of the tunnel. Because I am happy, that deep down in my soul kind of happiness. Because I have found peace. I cry because I am watching all of my dreams come true. I cry because I love myself. I continue to work each day in faith believing that what manifests in that day will fulfill my purpose and make the world a better place as I share myself, my gifts, and unconditional love with all who cross my path. This happiness, this peace, this joy is my wish for you. This is my work in the world and this is my constant prayer. This book is the next stage in the manifestation of that prayer.

Ase', Aho, Amen, Amen-Rha.

Introduction: My Story & My Journey

This book is intended to support you in answering two questions:

- How do I get on the road to becoming self-masterful?
- What does it takes to manifest what I want effectively and consistently?

If you have been looking for that something that has been missing or that has been holding you back from manifesting your dreams, your best life, your ideal lifestyle, living your purpose even after reading books like *The Secret* or taking online courses or going to motivational events, you have not been able to apply these principles to your daily life, then this book is for you. This book is for you if you have been searching for something that you can do that will make a real difference in your life. This book is for you if you are a person who wants to consciously create the life you want and make a difference in the world. This book is for you if you are serious about your development on every level and want to feel confident, happy, healthy, and know without question that there is no limit to what you can create for yourself and others.

It is my hope that by working with these human technologies in a tangible and practical way, you will build the muscles, the strength, and the capacity to make the world a better place by making your life better, thus making your corner of the world a better place as you create a better family, community and city. If we each work to change our lives and those close to us for the better, the world will be transformed.

I look forward to hearing your stories of transformation. I want to know the small shifts and big shifts in your thinking and your actions and how that changes your life step by step, decision by decision, action by action, thought by thought, like this technology has changed mine. It starts as a mind-shift and then as a shift in your actions and then as a shift in the way you create and the way you are, your very being. As you make use of this technology, you will see the impact and be able to intentionally use these technologies to manifest your vision from a good parking space to the lifestyle that you have always dreamed of and didn't believe you could have.

In my spiritual work, I have been practicing the technology of doing, creating and being, or the art of manifestation – visioning, managing my energy, controlling and focusing my thoughts and actions as well as the practice of gratitude. I was taught these technologies and I have been practicing them and working through all the lessons and learnings that it has revealed. It is the foundation of my first book, Life Mapping: A Journey of Self Discovery and Path Finding.

> It's so much about love.
> The love you have for yourself.
> The love you have for what you do.
> The love you have for others.
> The love you have for humanity.
> And the actions that love inspires.

The more I understood my purpose in this life and began to submit to the kind of consistent thought process and consistent action required to make my vision real no matter how big, the faster it began to manifest. And what I have come to understand is that to manifest that vision in this physical world, it takes the consistent use and application of these human technologies: Thought, Vision, Self-Awareness, Scanning, Strategy, Consistent Action, Relationship, Listening and Obedience.

Creation or manifestation is a natural part of human existence. We have the power to create in tangible form what we envision in our minds. Everything around us that is not found naturally in nature, humans have manifested. We manifest all the time both consciously and unconsciously. You have already been manifesting some of what you want. And for some of you it has been like shooting a shotgun in the dark and hoping to hit the target. You instinctively know these technologies and have learned how to use some of them. They have been helping you become more focused and clear about your intentions, thoughts and actions. This has given you the opportunity to accomplish more and make visible in tangible ways what you have envisioned in your spirit. I have traveled this journey as well, from self-sabotage to manifesting on a small scale, in a hit or miss fashion to now consistently manifesting my dreams and goals on every level. And in this book, I want to share that learning in an effort to support you to do the same.

Every human life is a spiritual journey. As humans we learn key lessons that allow us the opportunity to evolve and manifest our purpose in this lifetime. The challenge and beauty of being human is that we have a gift that sets us apart from other animals, **freedom of choice**. So we each get to choose in each moment to do good, to grow, to evolve, to fulfill our purpose or not.

From as early as I can remember, I continued to say yes to evolution, even when it scared me. I remember as a child getting scared and shutting down some of my gifts because in New Hampshire in the 70's the only information on spiritual gifts that I found in the library in my small town, was the Salem witch trials. Now that is very scary for a kid. I have spent the rest of my life trying to find that switch to turn those gifts back on. I could feel my spirit guiding me from New Hampshire to my family ancestral home in Louisiana, then to Howard University. But when I arrived in NYC for graduate school, my faith was challenged. Some powerful negative energy found its way into my dorm room. It was so intense that every day when I came back to my room from class, I would pause at the door, say a prayer and then open the door as if I expected someone to be there. My heart would race and I'd check the closets and under the bed before closing the door. I had limited knowledge about how to shift and transform energy at that time. I didn't know about crystals and herbs and smudging. I was terrified. I struggled for the days and weeks to come, although it felt like months. Then one night, I was awakened by this energy. My room was dark. The street lights from the city outside my window cast a shadowy glow around my room. I turned on a small light and began to cry from the fear. I reached inside myself to find the very thing that I needed and that had been used by my ancestors for generations, I found prayer. I prayed out loud to God asking him/her to protect me, asking that this energy leave my room and my life; and I made a promise to live a good life, to be faithful and to fulfill my purpose even though I could not articulate that purpose at the time. I cried and wailed into the night. Exhausted, I fell into a deep sleep and awoke refreshed. The sun was shining and the dark energy was gone. I was born again. This was my night of darkness and I emerged into the light.

That night I made the decision, the choice to evolve spiritually with intention. I chose to move in light vs in darkness. When I came out on the other side, I had new insights into my own psyche and behavior. I remember walking down East 110th St a few months later to my new Manhattan Ave apartment on the 5th floor of a 6 floor walk-up in Harlem and saying out loud, "I want to love myself exactly the way God made me." What that meant for me in the immediate was letting my hair grow natural and understanding what my hair looked like without a relaxer or any other chemicals to straighten my hair or that might change the texture. This was in 1983. For a Black girl, in the 80's, this was a big deal. My parents were plagued by fears of my not being able to get a job or be successful because I was sporting kinky, nappy hair which would be viewed as negative by the white establishment. I was unrelenting in my commitment. This was my second venture into the identity question of who am I. The first was at Howard where I absorbed Black History like a sponge from the never ending stacks of the famous Moorland-Spingarn Research Center in Howard's Library.

This decision, to learn to love myself, opened the gate to other decisions to both ask the Universe for support and to envision a life that was of my own making. And support came in the form of information, teachers, mentors, and life changing experiences. I am still on this journey.

My most profound teachers, outside of my parents, have both been named John.

The first John, is a wonderful black 1st nations man who came to Atlanta while I was working at a small house museum called Hammonds House Galleries for African Art in 1993. Hammonds House was the renovated historic home of Dr. Otis Hammonds, a physician and a great art collector and arts benefactor. A black man who envisioned his legacy continuing after his death by willing his home and art collection which became an art museum that quickly became a cultural gathering place. This was where I landed when I moved to Atlanta. It was perfect. At Hammonds House, people were always bringing flyers by for events and activities happening around town. One day, a flyer arrived about an upcoming sweat lodge. My co-worker and friend, Tamara, and I didn't really know what a sweat lodge was. There was no Google at the time. But after talking to the host, we decided to go. I remember saying, "Well, either something profound will happen or we will have a nice sauna. Either way it will be fun." Little did we know how true those words would ring. We went to the evening orientation, received our "job" assignment. I was a fire keeper. We brought the supplies required. I remember spending the night at Tamara's because she lived closer to the sight and we were supposed to be there really early in the morning. The leader, John, had come down from upstate NY to run the sweat lodge. He was and is a spry and strong man with bright sparkling eyes, almost elf like in his manner. Beaming with amazing energy. Happy and peaceful and wise. He put us to work tending fire, making soup, gathering wood, building the sweat lodge adding blankets and such. Everyone was busy. I was watching the fire, enjoying the scene and being in nature, when I looked up and saw hundreds, maybe thousands of Native American spirits coming up the hill into the backyard. When John came over, I said "We can start now, they're here". It turned out that this house was adjoined to a nature preserve that was an ancient Native burial ground. We started the traditional prayers and then went into the darkness of the lodge. By the second round, we simultaneously started using the dirt/mud created by the rainy day inside the lodge to paint our faces and when we came out after the second round we were astounded that each of us had done the same thing in the darkness. In the last round, we were all given signs and messages for our movement forward. I remember journaling for hours after the sweat lodge and talking intensively with John about my visions. We have been together ever since. He has supported my growth and development and life transitions for over 25 years.

Under his support, I have moved away from judgment, stopped looking so intensely for a guarantee for everything before moving forward, and learned to love and trust myself and find happiness and peace within and so much more.

The second John, I met in Cleveland. John D Carter, founder and president of the Gestalt Organizational Systems Development Center (Gestalt OSD Center for short). He was my teacher and mentor who is now a valued colleague and friend, as well. He is a powerful theorist, strategist, and practitioner. It was through the programs at the Gestalt Institute of Cleveland and the Gestalt OSD Center after they spun off from the Institute that allowed me to refine the way I work with human systems, i.e. organizations, groups, individuals, and taught me the language to describe things I had always seen in my work but had no language to adequately describe. The Gestalt training took my understanding of groups, organizations and the natural human process to the next level of mastery. And I learned about myself in ways I had never expected . My habitual patterns, my blind spots, the impact of incidents that happened in my past that were still impacting my decisions all came into focus. I began to heal my spirit and my emotions in new ways. I went into therapy. I participated in personal growth groups and did everything in my power to get my work done so I could heal and fulfill my purpose. By the time I got to Gestalt, I was already working with the Life Mapping practice. The learning helped me to know how to support others in their journey in a significant way.

I remember we'd sit in chairs in a circle. The beginning of these personal growth groups were always so slow as we did not know how to orient and move in a good way in the beginning. We'd all wait to see who would start something or do a piece of work. As the program progressed and I began benefitting from the work, I became impatient with this process. I remember announcing something like, "If ya'll don't want to work, I can do some. I have plenty and I want to get it done so if you don't want your turn, I can go" And of course that let the group off the hook. They were happy to learn from my work. That behavior got me labeled brave, courageous, but for me, I wanted to get my money's worth and I was committed to healing all those feelings and all that felt the least bit crazy inside of me. The more work I did the better I felt. I didn't feel special, just needy. My experience of myself was so different from how my classmates experienced me. This is a great example of multiple realities existing in the same space. Both experiences are valid and true. As I moved to master myself and expand my ability to hold the multiple truths that exist, these multiple realities could live in harmony with each other. That I was strong and courageous to my classmates became as real as my inner feelings of hurt and insecurity.

And with every step I felt better, stronger, clearer, happier, lighter, more lifted and I committed myself again to evolving, this time with the intention of *self-mastery*. I learned and I was invited to teach. And through Gestalt, I was afforded all manner of opportunities. I learned about my leadership ability and my impact. I spent time alone in the woods with my ancestors. I embraced by spiritual beliefs and I grew through my work with my colleagues and the women's group we formed, Wolf Creek. And I got clear about my life's purpose – to learn and teach unconditional love by supporting people to map their future and make their vision real. It was *Life Mapping*. The process I had been using and sharing for many years since I started my business and my first mentor and I had locked ourselves in the conference room that day in Newark to figure out what we wanted to do with our lives. And I mapped out an incredible vision of success, which I have been moving towards and away from and forgetting about and returning to for years.

There are so many people I have to honor and thank and remember for their profound impact on me, my life, and my work. It overwhelms me with gratitude.

The art and technology of doing, creating, and being is my learning to date. Shared with you so it doesn't have to take you 30 years to heal and move positively towards being healthy, happy and whole and living your ideal lifestyle.

Make note of your thought and new awareness:

Chapter One:
The Technology of THOUGHT

Human Thought is a powerful and creative force. Everything that man has ever done or created, started off with a thought. It's like a seed that gets planted in the mind that is nurtured and grows or is neglected and fades away. Again, we have a choice. We also get to choose what thoughts get attention and which ones fade into the ethers. It is our thoughts and our words that create our reality.

It is important at this juncture that we have a short discussion about the ego, the spirit, and the mind, because of the powerful influence and impact these parts of ourselves have over our thoughts.

The ego is the part of our system that attempts to control our actions. It was initially formed by us to protect us and watch out for us. It grows when it is fed fear, compliments, control, power, or when it is deprived of these things. The ego limits itself to what it can see and touch and control. Mostly it gets in our way and moves to block us when we begin to evolve, because as we evolve the ego loses its power and control over us. The act of evolution is not controllable. The ego also thinks it knows best and knows everything that we need. It is in direct competition with our spirit for our energy and attention.

Our spirit is directly connected to the Source of all, thus it has infinite potential. It has many intelligences or ways of understanding and knowing. The spirit can access information and knowledge from diverse sources if fed and nurtured. In western and modern society, the spirit is very neglected. What is nurtured in western society is the ego and the intellect. The systems for nurturing the spirit have been compromised or forgotten or labeled as heathen, and replaced with religion that has created a doctrine of power and control, fear and doubt as a strategy to keep people in their places, i.e.

lower than those who have been able to create our current system of class, power, and economics where men and money replace Nature as the supreme creator. These systems were designed in man's image and replaced the nature-based spiritually nurturing systems of indigenous people around the world and throughout the ages.

So our spirit gets neglected and our ego gets fed a diet of power, control, and fear. I remember falling into that trap in trying to empower and protect my children. I wanted to protect them from all that I could see in the world that was designed to harm them. And as a parent, I knew how I wanted to raise my children, i.e. to be healthy, happy, and whole and most of all free. I told myself that I wanted my kids to do things because it was the right thing to do and not out of fear. But I was submerged in fear and that was all I knew to teach them and the system perpetuated itself through me even though that was not my intention. So it is complicated and difficult to go against all that society has ingrained into us for multiple generations and do something different. But this is what we must do in the best way possible. Using these tools will help us. It takes consistent practice and focused action to learn to think, believe, and act differently from what society has taught us.

The technology of thought asks us to begin to control our thinking. Most people allow everything into their psyche and subconscious, allowing the ego to have total control of their thoughts. This destroys our power to create.

Here is an example. You watch a TV show about relationships, where the good looking man cheats on the woman and lies, then takes elaborate actions to keep his two women from finding out about each other, but they find out about each other anyway. You have conversations with your girlfriends who also have watched movies or shows where this happens. You have an uncle who cheated on your aunt. You hear other similar stories from your girlfriends. You feel abandoned by your father, because he is always working and you think maybe he's cheating on your mother. You begin to think, all men cheat. You encounter a man who has a powerfully attractive energy, he likes you and you like him. You begin the journey of a relationship. Automatically, when you can't get in contact with him you assume maybe he's cheating on you. You talk to your girlfriends about the situation. They have the same teaching and agree with you. You create a story in your mind and begin looking for evidence to confirm that story. You find a business card in his pocket with a woman's name and her cell phone written on the back in pen. Then your mind starts to race and create a new movie or story about this woman, your man, his cheating, etc. Then you start to beat yourself up about the head and shoulders with your thoughts – "I was a fool, I should never have gotten involved with him. I should have known better than to trust him." You share these thoughts with your girlfriends. They affirm your thinking and encourage you to make a plan to confront him. Now no matter what his explanation about the business card is, you think he's lying…. And your relationship is now doomed for failure. It has been poisoned. So whether he cheated or not, you can't hear him. Even if you decide to believe him, the water is tainted and you are now always on the look-out for any sign of him cheating. Your ego has created fear in your heart and hurt your spirit based on a lie that you created in your mind and allowed to grow and fester. This scenario plays out well for men with only a slight change in the pronouns.

When we let our mind go unchecked and the ego is allowed to control our thinking then we scare ourselves or make up the most undesirable scenarios and the Universe says, oh they keep thinking about this, that must be what they want. So the Universe joins us and answers our prayer to manifest those constant thoughts. And then here it comes and the ego says, "See, I knew this would happen."

After the election, I was sitting in the dentist chair, mouth propped open, listening to my dentist spin a crazy list of scenarios about what the new president was likely to do. I waived my hand for him to stop working. I said with cotton in my mouth, "Stop. Pay attention to your words. What you are saying is nothing that I am willing to agree to. No one knows what will happen." Don't allow yourself to go on these thought binges. All of your thoughts are prayers and the Universe answers all prayers. Your thoughts create your reality.

The Universe hears our thoughts and our words as prayers or requests. So every thought is a prayer and the Universe answers all prayers. Start thinking about your life and what you have incessantly thought about or been worried about and what manifests as a result?

It is important to control your thoughts so that you are creating only what you want and what is needed for your vision. Thoughts create words, words create your reality. This technology works and to get what you want requires mindfulness so that you are using these powerful tools - thoughts and words - wisely.

How do you begin to change your thinking?

First you start to **pay attention** to your thoughts and your conversations with yourself and others. Ask yourself: What am I creating with my thinking and my words? Is it contributing to or taking away from my vision of what I want?

Second, **interrupt** your thinking, especially if you catch yourself binge thinking - allowing uncontrolled negative thinking to happen. You have the power. Ask yourself… What is my intention with this line of thought? What am I creating? Is this what I want? If the answer is no, then ask: What do I want? And that will move your thoughts to what you want to create vs what you do not want.

Third, **focus** on what you want and when you catch yourself thinking negative thoughts, interrupt that negative thinking and replace those negative thoughts with thinking that supports your vision.

Chapter Two:
The Technology of VISION

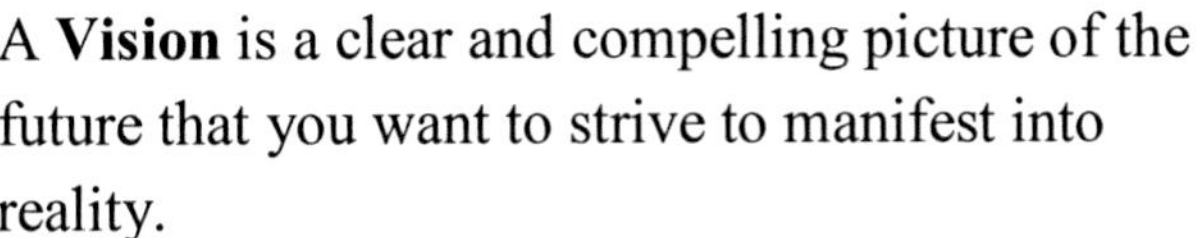

A **Vision** is a clear and compelling picture of the future that you want to strive to manifest into reality.

Your vision can be for your business or career or your life in all the aspects that are important to you. It is critical to have a vision, because we naturally ***move towards the pictures we create***.

So many people are helping others find their purpose and become clear about their vision. It is the starting point for any planning process or creative endeavor. I would venture to say every successful person you meet can talk about their vision. We look to leaders to articulate their vision. So what is all this talk about vision.

Why spend the energy creating a vision? If we move towards the pictures we create, then articulating a clear and compelling picture in our mind of the future that we desire is the first step to creating that future in our reality.

For me, a clear vision saved my life many times. It kept me from falling into a life of drugs and being taken advantage of so many times as I played at the boundaries of my insecurities, places where I was damaged and places that I was ignorant of the potential consequences of my actions. I was an 'at risk' teen and young adult by social work standards, but of course, I didn't know that. I was looking for freedom and self-expression and to find my own way. I teetered on the edges of danger without even being aware of it. I remember being in New Orleans for my first year of college. At the time I was 19 and on my own in the big city for the first time. New Orleans was an 8-hour drive from my parents by car and I was thrilled to be living in this magical city at the mouth of the Mississippi. It was my freshman year in college at the University of New Orleans. I had to move out of the dormitory at the end of the school year, and I had this great job with the 1980 Census (showing my age – yes, I am good and grown now). My college roommate's friend's brother came to my rescue and let me stay with him at his dad's house (I guess he was out of town or something) while I looked for an apartment. Eric. He was 30, unemployed and was selling a little "weed", I discovered later, to supplement his unemployment benefits. We became romantically connected. He was tall and lanky, a little goofy looking in a cute kind of way, and very attentive. He took me around and helped me find an apartment in the Historic neighborhood, described in the play, *A Street Car Named Desire*, at the end of what was now the Desire bus line on Desire Street. We fell "in love". He took me to work every day. And when they sent me out into the field to ask people to fill out their census forms without regard for my safety, he accompanied me into the public housing projects and all manner of neighborhoods. I would knock on the door just as sweet and naïve and he would stand behind me. I was blind to the potential dangers of my situation. Later I learned he was carrying his service revolver from the military, just in case. Afterwards, we would party in the French Quarter all night. I felt like I was living in a movie. But my vision was to become a famous movie star and I was headed to Howard University in August. There was no changing my vision of my future. When he said he loved me and wanted to marry me. I said yes. "When I graduate from Howard, we can get married and move to NYC where I will work in the theatre". I was so focused on my vision, I can't remember his response or his dream. At the end of the summer, we rode the bus to Shreveport so I could go home to get ready to go to Howard. Eric met my dad. My dad didn't like him and sent us to McDonald's to say our good-byes. What I know is that he never came to Howard to marry me. In fact, after a few months, I never heard from him again. I have no idea if he was lost, if he really loved me, or if I was being supremely manipulated and if he'd been successful he would have turned me "out" to a life in the streets or what. What I do know is that my feelings were genuine. And my vision kept me on track and safe and helped me make good decisions although I was a naïve, impressionistic, idealistic, young woman. The vision I had for myself changed over time as I learned more about my gifts and as new opportunities presented themselves. And I still remember that summer with fondness as a magical time. And my grown woman self knows that it was likely more dangerous than I could have imagined at the time. And I am grateful for the strength of my vision.

Creating a clear vision that is aligned with your values, your purpose, and your ideal lifestyle so you are moving with a congruent picture of your ideal future that feels right and good is one of the keys to your success. When I talk to successful entrepreneurs, they are clear about the role that vision has played in their success. When I coach those just starting to create their success, those who are able to get crystal clear about their vision move much faster toward success than those not willing to spend the time with themselves in order to clarify what they want.

When you take the time to make this picture clear, then you are able to make a clear request of the Universe. This is the ultimate co-creation. We are all being called to co-create with the Universal Energies of the Cosmos in very practical ways to consciously create the lives we desire (or unconsciously create the lives we hate). It's a choice.

Without your own vision, you are then subject to the whims and the vision and the energy of others. They may be living in integrity and their values may be aligned with yours and you may willingly join their vision. They may be creating their ideal life by fraudulent means or at the expense and freedom of others. You see these human systems all around us; created by powerful people with a clear vision that oppresses others so they can have all that they desire. This is the ego in its full power and glory.

When you choose to connect to the infinite power of the Universe with your positive intentions and your vision in light and love, you have the opportunity to create what you want in ways that also support and empower yourself and others, consequently building up the world and everyone in it. This is not just idealistic thinking, it is spiritual science – the rules of cause and effect, karma, and the law of reciprocity moving in action. This kind of thinking is based in the law of infinite abundance versus the scarcity model that so many people have been taught and operate in, which is grounded in an energy of power and control. Scarcity energy limits our abilities. Often those who control the institutions that teach that kind of limited thinking, don't even operate or believe what they are teaching us. But it is a strategy to keep us wanting and lacking. The Technology of Vision offers each of us the opportunity to begin to disrupt that energy and make a different choice.

The Technology of Vision asks us to keep challenging ourselves to take the time needed to create a clear and compelling picture of our future no matter how far away from our current reality it may be. A vision that inspires and energizes us to stay on our path and on task no matter what distractions may be set in our way. Applying the technology of vision to our lives means keeping our vision, our picture of the future in front of us, and choosing appropriate actions and making appropriate decisions by asking: Does this action or decision bring me closer to my vision? If the answer is yes, then do it. If that answer is no, then lovingly pass on the action, decision or opportunity. The technology of vision asks us to stay focused on what we really want and not be distracted by other "bright shiny objects promised by the world".

A clear vision will attract people who can help and support your moving forward. Some of those people will be there for the moment to bring insight, teach lessons, or provide important information that will support you on your journey. Others will test your resolve and your focus. Others will try to get you to follow the picture of their vision. You may choose to do this in the moment as part of your journey if you think that your two pictures align with each other enough to support your moving forward. In the best scenario, this becomes a wonderful partnership. In the worst case, this is a distraction that allows you to avoid the things you need to do. In these moments, discernment is needed so you learn the lesson that can move you forward.

Your vision is a touchstone that keeps you on track and can advance efforts more effectively towards your purpose and the impact you are here on the planet to create. Working until you can clearly articulate your vision is the work that makes this technology so very powerful and compelling.

Here are some examples of vision statements:

"To support a million conscious entrepreneurs to change the face of capitalism making it more accessible and available to everyone"

Move the Crowd
A strategic partner with MKM

"To support the self-mastery of the next generation to map their future and make their visions real"

MKM Management Consulting
My company

"To teach unconditional love in service of helping people to be healthy, happy and whole"

My personal vision

Now the story behind my vision is interesting. Because it answers the question of how do you come to this kind of statement. 'To teach unconditional love' came to me in a dream, a series of dreams actually. But it was a very clear message. When I gave birth to my first child, my intention as a mother was to raise my son to be healthy, happy and whole. I felt if I could do that he would be able to do anything he wanted with his life and fulfill his mission and purpose in this world. I recommitted to that same intention when my second child was born. That vision dictated my work as a parent along with my values of freedom, love, and spirit. I worked to instill a sense of compassion, integrity, and love into our relationship and our lives. I worked to protect them with the vigilance of an angry momma bear or fierce tigress. The other thing that happened, was in order to do that for my children, I had to do that for myself. You can't teach what you don't know. I had to move from fear and judgment to love. I had to heal and become healthy and whole. That too was a process. As a parent, I did the best I could to learn, to grow and to share that with my children, who are now adults, and help them to create and hold their own vision for their lives and learn their own lessons. I had to learn unconditional love – it required me to move away from judgment, to discern the truth, to love hard and love soft, to make hard decisions about my own life and my decisions about my relationship with my kids –what was acceptable and what wasn't. And a few years ago as I delved into my vision and purpose again, I began to understand that "happy, healthy and whole" was also part of my work in the world not just for my children. It was what the practice of *Life Mapping*, my first book, was attempting to create, it was what I was moving towards for my clients, both the individuals and the organizations. It was my version of making the world a better place. It was my personal mission and vision of my contribution to the world. It answers the question, WHY?

What is your vision of your contribution to the world? What is the thing you most need to learn yourself?

Chapter Three: The Technology of SELF-AWARENESS

Self-Awareness is honest knowledge of self, clarity about you, your identity, your thought process, your values, your triggers, your baggage, your intentions, how you perceive yourself and your environment, your impact (even when it doesn't match your intentions). Scanning your internal self, having the knowledge of self is a critical skill. The practice of self-awareness leads to growth and self-mastery.

This technology allows you to accept support and feedback so that you can see your blind spots. It increases your ability to process data about yourself and others. All of these aspects of self-awareness are critical for any kind of success. The more aware you are, the more you can move personal blocks out of your way so that your manifestation process is not sabotaged.

Self- Awareness is a big topic. It is a lifetime journey, not a destination, as we are ever evolving as human beings. This technology requires both quiet time alone and time spent interacting with others. It requires consistent reflection and scanning of your internal self and what is happening in the external environment that is impacting you or that you are trying to impact. It requires that you be in an observational stance with yourself and others, taking a step away from the situation so you can observe your own reactions, behaviors, intentions, and watch for the impact of your actions, words, energy on the environment you are interacting with. This observational stance, the act of self observation or stepping back, is what allows you to learn about yourself and see clearly who you are. It is also the key to making change so you can be more of who you want to be in order to create your vision.

It starts with a few simple yet complex questions.

- **Who am I?**
- **What do I want?**
- **What will it take to get what I want?**
    - What do I need to pay attention to get what I want?
    - Am I willing to do what it takes for me to get what I want?
    - How will I go about getting it?
    - What happened – what did I see, hear, observe (what is the data, not your interpretation)?
    - How did that make me feel?
    - What did I learn?
- **Who am I now?**
- **What will I do now?**

These questions can become your constant inner dialogue. You begin to see your own patterns and learn how you are or are not putting the technology into practice. You begin to see what is truly important to you based on observing your choices, actions and impact. You find out if what you say you want is a true want or something you think you should want or just a pipedream that would be nice if it fell into your lap, like hitting the lottery.

I remember working with groups of women back in the 90's when Bill Clinton funded welfare to work programs across the country. These particular women were in a Certified Nursing Assistants training program. We did a life mapping session about their vision and what it would take for them to reach their goals. We started with the "My Ideal Day" exercise. They loved it. It got harder when I asked, "OK. Now what will you need to do to make this ideal day your reality?" One woman talked about marrying a doctor and being a stay at home mom with all the luxuries she could imagine. Shopping, getting her nails done, out to lunch with her girls, fabulous home, car, the works.

Then it was about grounding that vision into her current reality. Her current kids, graduating from the program, then what? Then what choices do you make to make yourself attractive to that man and put yourself in a position to meet that man. Do you take the job at the hospital or the job at the nursing home? Do you continue your education and get your LPN or your RN? Do you become a nurse in the patient rooms or do you work to be in the operating room working next to the surgeon? What else do you need to do? Lose weight? Read certain books and magazines so you have the kind of knowledge and exposure to hold a conversation with that man who is educated and perhaps interested in a woman that is his equal? It was these questions that tested her vision and allowed her to put that ideal day into the dream or the vision category. It is the answer to these questions: To what do I need to pay attention to get what I want? Am I willing to do what it takes for me to get what I want? Do I grow and evolve or not?

I'm not judging. I have an "it would be nice to win the lottery" statement in my mind. And I have been willing to play the lottery a few times with an investment of about $20 a month in that dream. Of course, I know just what I will do with the money and when the Powerball is in the hundreds of millions, I revisit that dream. But that is all I am willing to do. I don't give it a lot of energy, I don't play every day, I won't spend a lot of money to make that more certain. I don't have a formula. It's more of a dream than a vision with a plan to make it real. But I play the lottery as a way to work on my own evolution of creation. How open can I be? How much money can I accept coming to me without this concept of work attached? So far, my biggest winning has been about $30. This is progress from only being able to accept $8. I choose to evolve. I am working on changing my mind.

On the other hand, when it comes to my business and my work with *Life Mapping*, my energy is different. I am willing to invest the resources needed. I am planning and taking action every day to achieve this part of my vision. I make the time that is needed to make it happen and I am not discouraged by the timeline as I consider this my life's work and the payoff is insignificant to the impact that I want to have. That dream has become a vision with a plan and is a priority in my life. It was this awareness that turned into a commitment, which became my contribution, my life's work. It is the cornerstone of all the work that I am doing with my husband, my friends, my clients, and myself. It is what fuels me.

Getting clear about what you really want is a big piece of self-awareness that shapes your life. Understanding where that want comes from and how your life's experiences are influencing you and your wants and dreams is critical in finding out how to find personal satisfaction, i.e. happiness. It also can point you into the direction of what needs to be healed in your emotions or your spirit or your body in order for you to get what you want.

My healing has been a journey, as all are. It started out with me acknowledging to myself that I was hurting and I was hurting for a reason even though I didn't know what that reason was at first. For me, my statement was, "I need to love myself just the way God made me" that sent me on my healing journey in an intentional way that was healthy and clear. Before that, I was self-medicating with alcohol, drugs and sex. I loved to party. But that satisfaction didn't last and it brought other issues that were not helping me heal or stay safe. And I was supremely blessed that I remained safe and nothing traumatic happened. I began to look at my

behavior, my choices, and my thoughts in a way that focused on my key question, "Is this helping me to love myself the way God made me?" I don't think I told anyone about my decisions. When they asked me why I was letting my hair grow natural, I'd say I want to love the hair God gave me. Then I started eating differently, moving towards healthier eating, I'd say I want to be healthy. When I cut back on my drinking and partying, I would simply say I have a lot to do tomorrow, I'm going home. This happened over years.
I journaled. I cried. And then slowly I met people who led me to the next step by giving me a book, recommending a workshop, or providing other information. Finally, I met my spiritual teacher and mentor, who guided my exploration of that question and pointed me to books and exercises and other resources that would support me.

That led me to make a more serious commitment. I eventually moved to Cleveland and learned about and had the opportunity to study at the Gestalt Institute of Cleveland and the Gestalt OSD Center. My intention was to get training to back up my instincts for working with individuals in *Life Mapping*. The training came with lots of self-awareness and ways to heal, and it was that healing and that moving into deep self-awareness and discernment and then into the deeper phase of self-mastery that became what was needed to do the work I really wanted to do. I needed to heal myself and work through my own issues before I could help anyone do their work. And I am still doing my work every day so that I am present and a clear vehicle to support others to do their inner work so they can live the life they have always wanted and make the contribution they are uniquely qualified to make.

Make note of your thoughts and awareness:

Chapter Four: The Technology of SCANNING

My mentor, teacher and the founder of the Gestalt Organizational Systems Development Center, John D. Carter, is fond of saying, that individuals and teams **"that can effectively scan their internal and external environment will outperform those who can't, every time".** This is because they will naturally be moving with the more complete "what is" picture or understanding of their current reality than those who are not effectively scanning. This awareness of themselves and their environment allows the individual or team to move and change their actions according to the shifts in the environment, in service of their vision and their goals.

The technology of scanning allows you to answer the question, "What am I paying attention to and what is needed now?" and move with that discernment.

Scanning is a skill that we all have. We are paying attention to something every time we walk into a room, every time we close our eyes, all day and all night in every situation. The effective use of this technology comes when we scan with awareness and learn what we habitually scan for and what we leave out. This is the other self-awareness piece; and as we develop and broaden our scanning ability, we will simultaneously develop and broaden our self-awareness.

Let's look at this a little closer. If you normally scan for emotional reactions for instance, then you are leaving out everything that is non-emotional: strategy, intellect, physical space, contradictions, etc. A lot is now missing in your picture of your current reality or your "what is" picture. If you only scan for those who agree with you, you learn nothing about what is happening with those who don't agree with you and what their issues or reluctance or ideas are. If you scan for obstacles, that is what you will find and you will miss the road that may be cleared for you to move efficiently and effectively.

So how do you broaden your personal scanning skills? First, begin to be aware of what you are scanning for and paying attention to in any given situation. Then you can discern what is missing from that picture. The awareness of why you do or do not pay attention to certain things can bring you to an understanding of your own patterns. Then you can choose more intentionally what you need to be scanning for that will support your intentions, i.e. to be safe, to know how to relate to a certain person or project, to make money, to help others. And those intentions will change as the situation and what you want change.

It reminds me of a story I have heard a few times, so I am not sure of the source. A person wants to help a homeless man. It is cold and winter so the person gives the homeless man a blanket. The intention was good. The impact was not the best, because now this homeless man has to spend time and energy protecting the blanket, carrying the blanket around, and he uses his limited energy on the blanket vs the things he used his limited energy on before like obtaining food and the other things that are critical for his survival. A fuller scan of the situation, such as having a conversation with that person might have yielded more information about the person's needs. Then the help offered might have been more useful with less unintended consequences.

The Technology of Scanning moves us away from making assumptions about any situation and gets us in the habit of seeking more information from a variety of sources to determine the most complete picture of our current reality. This allows us to move accordingly, because we will be able to see more fully the available choices.

Now, remember, any strength when overdone can become a weakness. Some people fall into the trap of continuous scanning and data collection, never moving into action because they don't have the complete picture. We move with the critical mass of information because we can never have all the information. We can never know everything. This is where faith and relying on a higher power gives us the impetus to move forward even when we have only a partial picture. Movement with intention that is based on data and our "what is" picture is called strategy. That leads us to the next technology.

Chapter Five: The Technology of STRATEGY

Strategy is focused action that allows you to move your vision in sync with the energy of manifestation. It offers the opportunity to move 10 giant steps forward vs the '2 up - 2 back' type of energy. It takes all the information at your disposal to discern the key actions that will move your vision forward. It requires all of the other disciplines to create and execute. Strategy allows you to discern the time and the timing of what you are creating. It creates a "go slow to go fast" phenomenon where you allow yourself to take the time to discern and then when the strategy is clear, the energy, momentum and action occur in rapid succession.

Strategy answers the question:

What key actions will allow me to move toward my vision given my current reality, my strengths and weaknesses, external opportunities and threats in a way that is aligned with my values?

I love brainstorming my choices in these moments. No judgment. Simply everything I can think of as an action that would move me toward my vision given everything I know. Then I look at the list and start to narrow down my options. Some ideas come off the list because those ideas go against my values. Some ideas come off the list because of resource limitations or the consequences that the action will create, or because although it might get me somewhere, I don't want to do it or I am not willing. (This is always a pause moment to explore why I don't want to do something or am not willing). Some come off the list because others will move me faster or farther towards my vision. And I might end up with 1-3 actions that make really good sense in the short term and in the long term. With that short list of key actions, I am poised to execute.

Let me demystify this technology I am calling: strategy in non-business terms.

A child is hungry and wants candy. Mom says no. The child cries. Mom still says no and offers an alternative food choice. The child digs its heels in – "No, candy". In this moment the mom has choices – what are they?

- Give the child the candy
- Give the child the food and when they get hungry enough they will eat it,
- Yell at the child (try using their power to make the child eat)
- Spank the child for saying no (punishment)
- Walk away
- Put the child down for a nap
- Go back to doing whatever she was doing prior to the request and the crying
- Talk to the child
- Negotiate with the child: if they eat the food they can get the candy

Which solution appeals to the mom will depend on her background and upbringing, her approach to child rearing, her religion, her values, her available time, her resources, her energy level (especially if she's considering getting into a power struggle with her 4 year old), her understanding of the child, her understanding of herself, her appreciation of the consequences of the different choices and the impact of those choices on her vision of the person she wants this child to grow up to be. On a good day that processing happens in a flash. On a bad day, the mom might fall into unconscious reaction based on her own habitual behaviors.

The child has choices. Listen and obey the mother, give up, fight for the candy, have a temper tantrum, negotiate. Even my four year old niece is negotiating with her mother. All of this depends on the personality of the child, their awareness, and the child's experience with the mother during their short lifetime, the state of the child's ego.

If the mother is aware and intends that the child listen and obey, then she may make the decision to stick to her statement without entering into a conversation or trying to negotiate with the child. If the mother's vision of the child is a highly engaged child that understands the rationale for parental decisions and the child's underlying choices and consequences, the mother might engage in a conversation about the candy, sharing what she is paying attention to, etc. Each choice may generate the same immediate results, no candy, but creates a totally different experience for the child. Each scenario teaches the child different lessons.

We make these types of decisions all the time about how we respond to any interaction or situation. Sometimes our reactions are conscious, intentional and thoughtfully considered. Other times they are instinctive and reactionary, or unconscious or less intentional. Sometimes our reaction is with awareness and sometimes not. You might need to slow down your reactions at first while you are developing the muscle needed to scan, see your choices, discern which choices will get you closer to your vision and make the best choice given the information you have and your awareness in the moment.

"We are always doing the best we can in any given moment" This is a gestalt-ism based in the observation that people will make better choices when they are able. Given the circumstances, our personality, the information and resources we have at our disposal, all of us will pick the best choice we can.

What are your choices to move your vision and ideal lifestyle toward becoming a reality? Which choices are strategic and will move you 10 giant steps forward? How do you want to move forward?

Chapter Six:
The Technology of RELATIONSHIP

The most amazing thing that has happened to me is receiving real support. To be seen and heard by another person is a powerful experience in itself. Then to engage with a person in a way that you are truly supported in your effort to be successful is amazing. I know this to be true from personal experience and I have watched as my clients and students have had that experience with me or others at the Gestalt OSD Center.

Most recently, I have had this experience in a way that I didn't expect and hadn't experienced before. The support came from two sources: (1) my coaches group at Move the Crowd and (2) my husband, Everett Gransberry.

I must say that building powerful relationships has not been the area in which I have felt strongest. And it has been in these two arenas, my coaches group and my marriage that I have begun to see those strong, reliable, authentic relationships manifest at a level that I found most gratifying.

You can't teach what you don't know. And my life experiences did not give me the ability to trust others, believe that I could depend on others to do what they said. I had a mantra that came from my 2nd Mom, Duchess, who often said, "if you want something done right, you need to do it yourself" That mantra or limiting belief had me twisting in the wind and unable to depend on anyone to help me because I was afraid they wouldn't do it, much less do it right. It took a lot to break through the blocks that this belief created in me. There was an underlying feeling that 'nobody wants to help me because I am not lovable or deserving.'

My mentors and teachers consistently said to me that I didn't need to trust others, I simply needed to trust myself. Easier said than done. As you can see, I had a lot of baggage in the relationship area. My parents divorced when I was 5 years old. My dad didn't always show up when he said, my mom didn't always let him (she was hurting). I missed him. I needed him. I was a tall, lanky teenager who was pretty, which often became a liability as many men don't have good boundaries and would project their sexual fantasies on me. Missing the primary male relationship in my life, I wasn't good at discerning good from bad. Growing up in the integration era of the South, school did not give me support, nor teach me to trust. And I was an artist and 'different', which brought its own set of dilemmas, as well. All in all, I found it difficult to get or accept support. And so when I heard the statement, "if you want it done right, do it yourself" I adopted it as my mantra along with "I could do anything I put my mind to" and I knew this to be true.

The other truth is that no one does anything alone. Everyone gets help. Sometimes we are aware of the help. Sometimes it is given behind closed doors and that person may never share their act of support and kindness.

But a relationship was created that was impactful enough for that person to support you in some way, even if it was only for a moment.

Sometimes you only need to ask. There have been plenty of times that young professionals have asked to shadow me or for me to mentor them. When the energy is right, if I liked who they were as a person, and I had time or a meaningful project, I would say yes. I have asked the same of others. I remember writing a letter to Woodie King Jr., founder and producer of the New Federal Theatre in NYC, asking whether I could carry his briefcase around and learn from him. In the 70s, he had discovered Ntozake Shange and was the first producer of her widely acclaimed play, *For Colored Girls When the Rainbow Was Enuf…* and then collaborated with Joseph Papp to take it to Broadway. He'd come to speak at Howard and I thought "WOW! I want to be a producer like him when I grow up." I want to work for him and learn. I wrote him a letter telling him I was coming to NYC, having been accepted into Columbia's School of the Arts Theatre Management program in 1983.

Our second year, we were required to do a professional internship. I went to Woodie right away. There were two of us and I was assigned as assistant to the producer and my classmate was assigned as assistant to the general manager. My first official mentor.

On a personal note, as much as I had trust issues, I desperately wanted to find a partner with whom I could build a life and a business and move in a significant way toward my big vision. What I didn't know until later is that I had to become or get ready for that kind of relationship. I was just like those ladies in the Certified Nursing Assistant training dreaming of their ideal husband. It wasn't until my first marriage was in trouble that I began the mantra that would change my experience of relationships.

I was determined to do everything in my power to make my marriage work and I started a new mantra. I would stand in the bathroom every day, twice a day and look in the mirror after I brushed my teeth and say… "I love myself." And I would cry. Then I would continue. "And I am in a mutually beneficial relationships that are respectful, caring, gentle, kind, sensual, sexual, spiritual, loving, monogamous,"….and any other criteria I could think of. I did this mantra for months, hoping it would change our relationship with my first husband because I had learned we create our reality. And if it didn't work, the mantra would call in the man that would treat me like this.

But what I noticed over time was that I changed. I became more respectful, more caring, more loving, kinder and gentler. My other relationships – my friendships and business relationships became more mutual. I was learning to be in relationships and do my part to be in good relationships. My relationship with myself shifted. I found that I wasn't crying anymore when I said my mantra. I began to love myself and believe that the vision for my relationship was possible and that I could create that kind of relationship. I had all kinds of opportunities. I was finally living in the same town as my father. And our relationship was growing. We were learning about each other and he was beginning to respect me as an adult. Eventually, I divorced my first husband as we grew more and more apart. The more I evolved and changed and the more he didn't, the more contentious our relationship became until the strain was too much for both of us. It was the hardest thing I ever did. But I continued to say this mantra for the next 10 years.

In 2012, I met my current husband, Everett. And in 2013, I joined Move the Crowd's coaching team. After a time, I came to accept the support and care from both the Move the Crowd team and from Everett. Now that love story is for another time. But what I will say is that his love, support and ability to create a vision with me, has created a powerful partnership that is allowing us to manifest all that we have been dreaming of. It has been an amazing journey. And having his support, has given me the ability to move more boldly into the full power of my vision. I know without question, he has 'my back'. And that is what I was yearning for and waiting for.

On the Move the Crowd side, I have gotten to experience a powerful work team that I can trust and rely on when I need support. Our commitment to the work, to supporting each other, accomplishing our individual and collective goals, and to working effectively is stellar. It has been an amazing journey watching Rha Goddess, the founder and CEO, build such an extraordinary team culture, one that fosters trust in our working relationship. Everything has not been only sunshine and roses, but there has been a commitment to working through whatever is standing in the way of our collective success.

Both these relationships have allowed me to move forward with the power to take my own work to the next level and to join others in doing, creating and being in authentic relationships that furthered our mutual visions.

Everett and I have been using these technologies to manifest our vision for our lives and relationship together. We created a life map as a couple to support that vision. And it has made all the difference.

The technology of relationship rests in the power of the collective. It is grounded in the power of the statement **"when two or more come together in agreement, it is done".** This is my version of the biblical quote about agreements. When you build powerful relationships where you can share your vision without restraint or judgment, and there can be mutual agreement, then it is done. It will manifest so much faster than when you hold your vision alone.

Building powerful relationships is essential, be they life partners or business partners who believe in your vision and your ability to manifest it, or be they people who arrive just for a moment or a season. We all need people with different gifts at different stages in our development. Some will only need to agree with you for the moment, some people will bring you critical information; some will honor you with a life-long relationship. Others may be critical of you, yet if you listen carefully you may discover new information hidden in their judgment. This can help you grow and strengthen your commitment to what you are creating.

Discernment is needed with all relationships in order to maintain good boundaries and know when to move on and when to stay. Honor all the people who come to you in support of your vision and the role they play. Love and bless them for their contribution, no matter how big or small. These relationships are critical – ideally they will be mutually beneficial as you share your gifts with others. Value and hold sacred those life partners that are put on your path to teach you and who agree to support your vision. They are heaven sent.

Humans are communal beings. We thrive best in mutually beneficial and positive communal relationships. That is what inspires us to build and live in families and communities, even when they are virtual. It is through shared and authentic contact and interaction that has depth and substance that allows us to build powerful relationships. It is when we learn about each other, our vulnerabilities, our life experiences that we develop compassion and mutual respect and the ability to move beyond our own personal critics to support the other in their needs and wants. It is then that we are able to trust and allow ourselves to be supported in all of our strengths and our vulnerabilities.

Don't miss out on this important human experience. If you want to attract like-minded people with whom you can build community, you want to be clear about what it is that you want from them and what you are willing to give. Spend time to get clear and be honest about your intention and where that intention is coming from. Create a mantra to support you.

Learn to give the thing you want most to receive without attachment or expectation and then watch the Universe deliver the exact relationship(s) you need to make your vision a reality.

Chapter Seven: The Technology of CONSISTENT ACTION

Consistent action is the technology that builds and creates the tangible aspects of your vision. This consistency gives you the ability to do what is needed now, while you continue to scan for information about future needs that will help you to change your world.

Consistency is the key to success whether your commitment is to a healthy lifestyle, your word, your partners, your scheduling, your work, your communications, your needs, or all of the above.

Consistency allows you to become masterful. It's the 10,000 repetitions that makes what you do look as seamlessly easy as brushing your teeth. It is consistent action that brings mastery to your craft and produces tangible results.

So many people want overnight success. However, when you listen to the stories of successful people, that overnight success was 10 years of consistent action when no one was looking. Consistent action is the 'doing' part of these technologies. It comes after the thought, the vision, the language. It puts your self-awareness, your scanning and your strategy into action that makes the vision you have held in your spirit, your mind and your heart a reality. It is the tangible work.

When I coach folk about how to create their vision, their ideal lifestyle, I encourage them to talk about their future actions. When they are at the peak of their success, what do they want to be **doing.** It is your actions that show you who you are. Want to change who you are, pay attention to your thoughts and then change your actions.

In the theatre, they say, "fake it 'til you make it". Act successful, do the things successful people do until you can do those things with ease.

So how does that look in its application. You want to be a writer, write stuff even if no one reads it. If you want to make money, do things that make money. If you want to find your life partner, go out and live your best life so you are in a position to meet that person, because you are being the person you want to be. If you want to help others, find a place that you can use your special gifts and talents to help people. If you are meant to make money at it, you can get help figuring that out once you clearly see the value that your help brings and you master the activity that you want to share. Sometimes you are destined to make a living at your purpose. Sometimes you have that good paying job so that you can fulfill your purpose by volunteering outside of work. Be open to the Universe's instructions and get busy doing whatever that thing is.

Make note of your thoughts and awareness:

Chapter Eight: The Technology of LISTENING

Listening happens on many levels. It's more than hearing the words someone is saying or not saying. The technology is the art of listening deeply into intangible levels of awareness and consciousness. This kind of listening requires you to be grounded and to shuttle your attention to the various levels of your internal self and the various levels of your external environment. This concept is the most difficult to describe.

Listening also happens with more than just your ears. It happens with your eyes, your skin, your energy, your heart, your head, your gut, and your spirit. It is real observational data or information such as words, body language, energy, aura, etc. And it is intangible information that takes some time to understand or know how to process.

The Technology of Listening teaches us new ways of processing that helps us discern intent from impact, reason from emotion, hurt from rhetoric, commitment from promises, past from present, love from lust, and more that doesn't even have words. The discipline of listening to your spirit is the key to determining what is needed at the moment when information is sketchy. It allowed our ancestors to survive in the *wilderness or in the new world*. It is this kind of listening that connects us to all things.

If you imagine that when you were in the spirit world before you were born, you had access to all the ancient, current and future knowledge ever conceived. When you choose your parents and agreed to the lessons you needed to learn for your next level of evolution as a spiritual being, you were then conceived and went into a deep sleep. You forgot all that you knew including your purpose in the life you were coming to live.

Then we are born. Our connection to the spirit realm decreases with each day until the veil between those worlds is closed. Then we spend the rest of our days on the planet trying to reconnect with the spirit world enough to complete our task during this lifetime and get back to perfection. As we move to be more conscious and to develop to the next level of evolution, we have the opportunity to regain some of the skills that allow us to tap into the spirit realm and access information that most of us don't even know exists. We get little encouragement from the Universe as we become more aware and begin to listen. Every time you experience "de ja vu", it is your intuition becoming stronger. Some people hear the voices of their ancestors guiding them. Some feel the presence of spirits or angels. All of this is a demonstration of deep listening. I remember the first time I heard my ancestor guides say my name. It was a breakthrough in my ability to listen at new levels.

Putting the technology of listening to work in your life means you are spending time each day alone in silence and learning to be comforted by the silence. It means during that time, like in meditation, you are not thinking or in dialogue with yourself, but are listening to your spirit, which is that place inside each of us that speaks to us without words. It is the place of knowing. It is the essence of the self and our connection to the spiritual realm. This is the place I go when I have no answers. When my intellect fails me and I don't know what is needed next.

On an interpersonal level, putting listening to work, allows you to take in what the other person has to say vs listening for your turn to speak. It allows you to swallow as you take in the other person fully and feel the impact of their presence and their words and their actions. It allows their words or actions to impact you before you respond. This is especially important to practice and teach children, to practice with partners and spouses, family members and friends, those whom we love and respect. It is a good practice in heated discussions when finding solutions is important to each person. It is an important process when looking for the truth among all the rhetoric and noise in the world.

Listening is also a way to get grounded and connected to yourself. It is what is needed when you ask the Universe a question. Listen for the answer.

The more you listen, the more you will hear.

It is through the technology of listening that you can discover what you want (vision), what you are willing to do to get it (values/commitment), how you will go about getting it (strategy, consistent action), and the time and timing of your actions.

Listening is a way of being.

Make note of your thoughts and awareness:

Chapter Nine: The Technology of OBEDIENCE

It takes time to train the ego to submit and surrender, to listen and obey. **Obedience** is often defined as taking action under the orders of an authority figure. For this book, I want to amend this definition. The Technology of Obedience is about obeying your spirit, intuition, your purpose; your inner knowing, that place inside that has no words or sound. It is your inner authority that you are learning to listen to and obey.

We are always asking the Universe for answers. It is equally important that after you ask, after you listen and discern, when you receive that answer to your question; that you obey.

That means doing what is being asked of you, even when you don't think you have the capacity or the knowledge or the strength or don't feel worthy. Obedience is the act of saying yes to the Universe's request and following through.

> *"When you walk to the edge of all the light you have and take that first* ***step*** *into the darkness of the unknown, you must believe that one of two things will happen. There will be something solid for you to stand upon or you will be taught to* ***fly****."*
>
> *Patrick Overton*

I began to practice listening and obeying about 10 years ago. My mantra became: "Listen and Obey". For me it meant to act. To do it without questioning or hesitation or proof or a guarantee. This was difficult for me because I had been asked to provide guarantees all of my life. And looking for a guarantee was my biggest life block. The thing that I most needed to learn. It was the thing that kept me from doing, creating and being my full self.

At first, I would listen and get nothing. Then it would be like a quiet whisper that was so fast that I often missed it. I'd be driving and the thought would fly through my consciousness to change lanes or turn left, and by the time I realized the instruction, it was too late and I was stuck in traffic.

Sometimes I could feel the Universe trying to answer my question and I couldn't understand the answer. I would feel stuck, frustrated. When I finally learned to listen, I began to feel a sensation that was usually around my shoulders and right ear, which alerted me to pay attention. At first, I knew I was getting a message, although I couldn't understand it. I knew something was happening. Then I finally heard my name. "Monika". It was clear. I'd made a huge breakthrough.

Now my goal has became to listen, know, trust, and obey. When I am coaching and I get that sensation, I listen and whatever intervention or question comes, I voice it. It has been an incredible experience and gift.

Interpersonally, I have practiced listening and obeying my husband. This requires trust and great respect. I trust his instincts. I know he is always scanning and looking to protect us, so when we are out and he says let's go, or moves me behind him, or asks me to do something, I listen and obey immediately. If I don't understand what is happening, I ask him about it later. Then we discuss the situation together after it's over and when there is no danger. In this way, no issue is created in the moment, because I didn't obey. It was what I was trying to teach my children for many years.

Obedience requires you to completely surrender your ego and submit, not to the person, but to the Universe. The Universe is guiding you via your own spirit or the spirit of someone else. When you hear someone say duck, or tells you to leave or wait in the car, obeying without thought or hesitation can save your life.

In our Western mindset, obedience is labeled with all kinds of negative connotations. It brings up all the ways people have used this concept to oppress others and bend them to their will, often with traumatic consequences. For me, because of my family legacy of slavery and the suppression of women in the US and globally, it was even more difficult to accept the need to obey. I was in a warrior stance to protect me and mine. I had unexplainable fears of people harming me and my children and my spouse. So much baggage in my DNA from the experience of my ancestors, both black and Native American in this country. The Women's liberation and African liberation movements, and the civil rights work of my parents, brought the tangible history of my experience into stronger focus. For these reasons, the idea of obedience was not in my repertoire. You can think about your own heritage and point to reasons why you personally may have resistance to the concept of obedience.

However, once I had children, I wanted them to obey me, because I was literally trying to keep them safe. Since I have been practicing and using this technology, I have come to have great respect for the practical applications of obedience and the role of men and the role of women in history relating to its application.

Originally, when women walked behind the man, it was so that the man could take the bullet or the sword. The woman walked on the inside of the sidewalk in Europe and in early American settlements, because there were no sewers and all manner of things would be thrown out of windows into the gutters. It was for her protection. And she protected him and the children in her care in the same manner. Children were to listen and obey so they could learn, and be safe. There was supreme respect in ancient cultures for this kind of knowing, teaching and practice.

Our modern world is noisy and the ego is given power that keeps us from hearing what the spirit or the Universe is saying in answer to our own deeply needed questions. So this technology of obedience is a way to move with spirit that is mostly foreign to us and our parents. And it is what we are longing to get back to – that deep connection to ourselves, our spirit, nature, and the Universe itself.

Knowing - Not looking for words that can be heard and repeated, but the understanding comes with that special feeling without words that gives you certainty. Then obeying that knowing, by moving into action.

Listening and Obedience is the technology that brings us into harmony with Nature and all living things. It is the technology of BEING.

The Application

Practice these technologies in any order you are called to do them. Take one or two at a time and practice, concentrate on them and put them to use in your life. Then when you are ready to manifest, use the following agreement process with yourself and a partner.

> *When two or more are gathered in His Name... It is done.*

This is a manifestation and agreement process that puts all the technologies to work on your behalf. It was taught to me by my spiritual teacher as his teacher taught it to him.

It only takes a few minutes and it is extremely powerful.

Step 1: Surrender

In your own words state your surrender to the Universe

> Ex. "I know there exists a source greater than me. I know there is an energy that can lift me up beyond what I can imagine. I surrender to that source of all knowing."

Ask your partner to agree and state his/her surrender then you agree with your partner

Step 2: Believe

State what you believe

> Ex. "I believe in the divine energy that is God."

Ask your partner to agree and state his/her belief.

Step 3: Accept

State what you can accept

> Ex. "I am willing and ready to call in and accept what is needed."

Ask your partner to agree and state what they can accept and you agree.

Step 4: Change

State that you are ready to change

Ex. "I am ready to change. I know that to do this next thing I must change and I am willing to change."

Ask your partner, "Can you see me changing?"

They say, "I can."

Ask your partner to state that they are ready to change and you agree in the same manner.

Step 5: Petition

State your petition/request

Ex. "At this moment I would like to become the most energetic medium possible."

Ex. "At this moment I would like a million dollars."

Keep it simple - ask only for the thing you can accept, one thing at a time.

Ask your partner to agree and then state their petition and you agree.

Step 6: Know

State what you know

This is a statement of what you can accept and believe.

Ex. "I know that XYZ will happen. I can feel the energy moving and I will realize what I am asking for very soon."

Ask your partner to agree and state what they know and you agree.

Step 7: Give Thanks
Each person gives thanks for what they have asked for as it is already done.

For once you offer this process, your request is done in the spirit world, and it is your job to wait for it to manifest in your reality without questioning that it will.

Summary of Learning

Mastering these technologies doesn't have to take a lifetime. The attempt to master these technologies makes miracles possible. The mastering of these technologies takes you to new levels of self-mastery. Self-mastery allows you to navigate your environment and to create a life for yourself that is perfectly suited for you. No matter what. Period. No ifs, ands, or buts. Without question. You can chose to live your ideal life. I can testify to that. You can manifest all that you will need to create your vision and make it real. This is the promise.

The rest is a choice. The choice to open your mind, to quiet the ego, to listen to your spirit. The choice to practice and learn and evolve, using these technologies. The choice to use these technologies to do good in the world or not. The choice to create your vision in a good way or not. The choice to create a life for yourself and those you care about that is happy, healthy, and whole, or not. This is the human dilemma. This is the power and freedom of choice.

We all have this choice in each moment of our lives. We can make good choices or bad. We can create heaven on earth, if we choose to. It's up to us. What choice will you make? What kind of world will you create with your thoughts, your vision, your actions. How will you use the gift of scanning, self-awareness, strategy, listening? Who will you obey? What will you create? Who will you become?

Thank you for allowing me to share these insights with you. My affirmation is that you will move in a positive way on your journey and you choose to evolve and move towards self-mastery. And like the butterfly, transform.

About The Author: Monika K. Moss-Gransberry

Monika Kathleen Moss-Gransberry is a self-mastery coach. She is celebrating 30 years in business, as founder and president of MKM Management Consulting. Monika is the mother of two, stepmother to three, grandmother to 6, auntie to 4, play mother, mentor, coach to countless young adults, entrepreneurs and leaders. She is a wife, daughter, big sister, friend and lover of spirit and beauty. She is a student of Gestalt, systems, people, history, spiritual practices, and herself. She is a "practice what you preach", "keep your word", "be free" kind of woman. She holds deep respect for nature, the planet, animals, and human beings. She is pro-black, pro-women, pro-men, pro-people of color, pro-youth, pro-elderhood, pro-individual choice, pro-community, and pro-spiritual beings, a freedom fighter and a spiritual teacher.

Monika is third generation out of American Slavery, proud granddaughter of Frank Moss, Lorenza Webber Moss, Katherine Hill Bowen, CD Hill, James Bowen. She is the proud daughter of May Katheryn Haugstad, Paul Haugstad, Donald T. Moss, Camilla D. Moss, Bernice Robinson, Nina Simmons, Sy Simmons, and numerous adopted parents, mentors, and play mammas. She is second generation HBCU graduate (from Howard University), and Ivy league graduate (from Columbia University). She is a proud artist, producer, thespian, writer, teacher, consultant, creator and agreement partner. She is an eternal learner and searcher of self-mastery and spiritual consciousness.

Other published works include:

- Life Mapping: A Journey of Self Discovery and Path Finding
- Embracing Cultural Competency: A Roadmap for Nonprofit Consultants (contributor)
- And numerous articles, blogs, and ruminations.

Make note of your thoughts and awareness:

Make note of your thoughts and awareness:

Make note of your thoughts and awareness: